Suffering:
The Unwanted Blessing

SUFFERING
THE UNWANTED
BLESSING

by
FRANCES
HOGAN

Collins
FLAME

William Collins Sons & Co. Ltd

London • Glasgow • Sydney • Auckland

Toronto • Johannesburg

First published in Great Britain in 1990 by Flame

Flame is an imprint of
Collins Religious Division,
part of the Collins Publishing Group
8 Grafton Street, London W1X 3LA

Copyright © 1990 by Frances Hogan

Printed and bound in Great Britain by
Courier International Ltd, Tiptree, Essex

CONDITIONS OF SALE

The Unwanted Blessing

Jesus called the people and his disciples to him and said, "If anyone wants to be a follower of mine, let him renounce himself and take up his cross and follow me. For anyone who wants to save his life will lose it; but anyone who loses his life for my sake, and for the sake of the gospel, will save it. What gain, then, is it for a man to win the whole world and ruin his life? And indeed what can a man offer in exchange for his life?" (Mark 8.34–36).

There is no more unwelcome message in the modern age than to be told to take up your cross. Everyone wants to shed their cross, dump it, hide it, cure it, talk it out, but not take it up and carry it. That's the last thing on earth we want to hear. Many people go to healing services for the express purpose of shedding their cross, and they think that there is something wrong with the healer when nothing happens. This is especially so when they see someone else receive healing and relief when they are left with their problem. "What is wrong?", they ask. Why should I have to suffer? I'm no worse than anybody else: why should it happen to me? How can God be a good God and let this happen? Why does He not intervene to stop it? Is there a God at all? And they begin to question everything they ever believed in. This questioning is not a bad thing if it leads to the true answer to suffering.

THE UNIVERSALITY OF SUFFERING

It takes very little observation to conclude that suffering is a universal phenomenon, whether it is seen from the individual or national viewpoint. People from every walk of life suffer in different ways, for neither sickness, tragedy nor death are respectors of persons. They visit the high and mighty as readily as the hovels of the shanty towns of the world. They come uninvited and unwanted by all. They are not impressed by a person's station in life: they cannot be bought or sold, manipulated or controlled, although political leaders like to give the impression that they can control everything. Yet so many "Acts of God" give the lie to their claims. Whole nations languish in the grip of injustice, war, famine and disease, which even worldwide relief agencies seem powerless to control. The problem seems only to get bigger.

On the individual level suffering comes in many varied ways, even if we are lucky enough to have plenty to eat, are in sound health, and living in a country with a reasonably sound economy. Suffering is meted out at the hand of others, either intentionally or otherwise. There is the almost inexplicable mystery of man's inhumanity to man, seen at all levels of society and in all walks of life. In the rush to make "our first million" we may walk over many others along the way, discard those people who are not "useful", buy the friendship of the "great" while manipulating or controlling the weak ones. In this drama of everyday life we may find ourselves either the oppressors of others or the oppressed. In this sense suffering is not given to us by God, but by our fellow humans. Our cross is our neighbour whom we are challenged to deal with every day according to justice, charity and forgiveness.

WHAT IS OUR CROSS?

Our cross is the whole burden of being a fallible human

being in a sinful and sinning world with all the consequences of this. It is the acceptance of oneself and others warts and all! Acceptance too, of our talents or lack of them; of the responsibilities of work, or trying to cope with its absence. My cross is the whole burden of my sin and failure to live as a disciple of Christ should. It is the defects in my character and personality that must be submitted for help, healing and transformation. It involves the whole conglomeration of hurts and sensitive areas due to past experiences that were painful, even painful to remember. It's all the "no go" areas that make living with me difficult for others. It's the burdens and responsibilities of life, even the sheer monotony of everyday living that is not at all glamorous, and it involves all the duties of my state in life, with its burdens and joys.

Our cross also comes from other people with whom we live and work. It's the acceptance of them also, in all their reality, as they present themselves in everyday life. We brush up against their faults and failings too, and discover that others do not understand us for the simple reason that they are different from us, in character, personality, upbringing, giftedness, and outlook on life. As well as bringing richness to one's existence this can bring pain too. The cross also embraces the accidents that happen to us, uninvited and unwanted, it is true. Take for example the driver sitting quietly at red traffic lights waiting their turn to drive on: the driver behind approaches the lights too fast crashing into the peaceful neighbour ahead. Is this accident sent by God or by one's neighbour? God does not destroy what He has made and redeemed, but the neighbour is different. The cross is the neighbour who came to you when you least needed it, and gave you problems you would never ask for.

Even on the homely level of relationships in the family how much suffering can be found! Witness the pain of parents as they agonize over the behaviour of their children. How much heartbreak there is in the infidelity of a spouse. To be betrayed in love, and by so-called love, is to be outraged at the core of one's being. Yet millions of adults live with this pain today, and children also, who are forced to choose between one parent and another when those who loved them most brea ⸱ up their centre of security in the home. How many young families have suffered the loss of a parent through death when the children are at their most tender age? Many break up mentally and emotionally under the strain or fall victim to illnesses that medicine cannot control or heal.

There are times when we say that a person "has a very heavy cross" to bear, when we observe an unusually great sorrow in their lives, perhaps the long illness of a family member, or the heartbreak of a handicapped child, or the dreadful tragedy of the loss of life due to drugs, rape, suicide or murder, just to name a few. In such cases we wisely do not advise those who are plunged into an abyss of suffering. We just walk by their side lovingly supportive, listening, praying and compassionately "being there" for them. For what can we say in the face of such irreparable loss! Such inexplicable burdens? We must allow the sufferer to find their way as we quietly help them to carry their cross, not by being pious, or by being a "Job's comforter" giving all our theories and reasonings that make no sense in the face of terrible pain, but by imitating Simon of Cyrene who wordlessly helped Jesus carry His dreadful burden to its conclusion on Calvary. However,

I do not think it possible to help another person to carry their cross if we do not even recognize our own, let alone carry it!

Since we could go on, let us sum up: the cross is a combination of factors coming from within oneself, but also coming from our brushing up with other people in everyday life. It also includes all the factors in national and international life which are outside our control, including so-called "Acts of God". Since this is so, it is now clear why it is a fruitless exercise to try to run away from one's cross, to hide from it or to shed it. To do so is to refuse to live: to choose non-life which leads to emotional and spiritual death, and to refuse the challenge of living on Planet Earth as a fully alive person, one who leaves their footprints in the sands of time.

IS THERE A SOLUTION, OR EVEN A MEANING TO THIS?

Those who are plunged into an abyss of sorrow cry out for meaning to their experience. This message is not aimed at those who have not suffered, who have not been tried and tested by sorrow and pain. They can afford to theorize and come to "book" solutions, as Job's comforters did, only to be proved wrong by life experience. This message is for those who suffer from one who has walked this road for most of life, and has found that the solutions offered had actually worked, right through to victory and joy. It would be cruel to offer unworkable solutions to those who suffer, for that would lengthen the path of pain. When suffering and sorrow visit us there is only one choice: breakdown or breakthrough, for suffering can destroy, just as it can heal and redeem.

I have always felt terrible pain at the news of a suicide successfully carried out. My heart cries out: but where was your neighbour? Was there no one to listen to your pain? Did no one in your environment have an answer to life? Where are the Christians? The suicide tells us that no one offered anything to live for. The solutions were not worth the effort. Their death is an accusation to us all, and a terrible challenge to reach out to others we meet on life's journey.

The fact of suffering and sorrow is known to everyone, but the meaning of suffering is known to very few, I do not know why. The value of suffering and its grace-filled opportunities for growth in grace, and especially its redemptive power is known and grasped by so few that we need to proclaim it from the housetops. The message I have for you is that there is a way through even if you do not get healed physically, and you appear to be saddled with a problem that others misunderstand, and even accuse you on its account. Some Christians think that being a follower of Christ means being trouble-free, but they did not get this teaching in the gospel: quite the opposite in fact! It may be the influence of our society which demands a pain-free existence. But a pain-free life is impossible for one who wants to live a responsible life within the family, within the community of the parish, town or country.

Our generation keeps searching for the magic pill that will drown the effects of our bad or irresponsible behaviour, so that we will *feel* good. Its the de-caffeinated coffee mentality. Drink the coffee but don't suffer its effects. Have your sexual pleasure without its responsibilities. Smoke your low-tar cigarettes. In other words: have your cake and eat it. Yet the evidence abounds that we can drug a dying patient so that they don't feel any pain, but they die anyway! The magic pill takes away the *feeling* but not the *fact*. It dehumanizes us. A whole generation of young people have fallen victim to this idea. They get hooked on drugs which drown all pain so that they live an unreal euphoric existence for a time, that is until the magic pill shows its fangs in its side effects: it kills. It's a death drug and we must tell them that. The very refusal to feel is a refusal to live. They kill themselves emotionally before they kill themselves physically, while causing heartbreak to everyone who loves them. The "drown all pain" drug is no solution: it's part of the problem, as is anything that does not permit us to function as we were created with mind, heart, body and the most neglected part of our being: our spirit.

Someone, somewhere, with great patience, will have to rehabilitate this generation back to the pain of being human, to the acceptance of being a fragile, weak human being in a world full of wonder, challenge, need and suffering. They will have to return to feeling and the possibility of compassion. In this return journey they must be made to face their fears and deal with their anxieties so that they can grow and mature. They will have to learn to tolerate suffering, for to be human is to suffer! In other words, they must take up their cross and carry it.

Pain is one of our God-given gifts, a signal for us to take care of body and soul needs that might otherwise be neglected to our undoing. Pain is the red light that says to us: "Stop, look, listen! What's going on?" Just as you need your car serviced, perhaps you need your body serviced by a doctor now? Perhaps it is soul pain? Have you neglected your inner life? Soul food and body food are very different in nature, and many are confused when after the body has been well taken care of, their inner cry is still there. It says, "I want something, and I don't know what I want". It's a gnawing dissatisfaction at gut level that will not go away unless soul food and soul medicine are given. It is tragic that so many can no longer even interpret this cry from within, for their soul has been neglected for so long that it has become the prisoner of the body, a prisoner whose cries are drowned in alcohol, sex, drugs, hyperactivity, depression and so many other things. I believe that this neglected cry is the source of so much unnamed suffering today in our Godless society.

THE TEMPTATION TO RUN AWAY

When faced with the possibility of suffering the instinct of all is to run away. This is well expressed in Psalm 55.6–9:

> O that I had wings like a dove
>   to fly away and be at rest.
> So that I would escape far away
>   and take refuge in the desert.
>
> I would hasten to find shelter
>   from the raging wind,
> And from the destructive storm, O Lord,
>   And from their plotting tongues.

The psalmist was suffering from personal betrayal by a trusted friend. Whan an agony! In his pain his eyes were opened to the treachery that lies everywhere that sinful human beings live and work. Until now he knew this by hearsay, but it did not touch him, but now that he is torn apart by his present suffering he sees pain everywhere. This is a common experience for sufferers.

> "I see how Violence
>   and Discord fill the city;
> Day and night they stalk together
>   along the city walls.
>
> Sorrow and Misery live inside,
>   Ruin is its inmate;
> Tyranny and Treachery are never absent
>   from its central square"
>
> (Ps. 55.10–11).

For anyone whose eyes are open, sorrow and suffering can be seen everywhere. These two life-companions rarely leave us, especially if we desire to live adult, responsible lives, and particularly if we wish to participate in solving the needs of the seething masses of humanity who labour under war, disease, famine, inequality, discrimination or persecution of any kind. We can only escape suffering by refusing to live, and this in itself puts us in the problem camp, where others will have to bear the burden of trying to carry us through life.

How can anyone live at peace with themselves in a life of self-indulgence and luxury when their suffering neighbours from all over the world cry out to them from their TV screens for pity and help? In other words how can we play the part of the rich Dives in the gospel when poor Lazarus lies at our feet? Jesus condemned Dives for his neglect of the suffering of his neighbour, not for the fact that he had money and means. He found himself in Hell because he shut his eyes to the plight of others less fortunate than himself (see Luke 16.19–31). The rich West is Dives, I believe, to the starving Third World. There is no escape from the agony of this responsibility.

The temptation to run away from our own pain and the pain of others is real, but it is no solution. Running away is the coward's way out – but who has not tried it, at least once? Who has not tried to sweep the problem under the carpet hoping that it would go away? Who has not put it on the long finger, saying: "Oh, I will deal with that next week", but next week never comes? Who has not hoped that a good night's sleep would solve everything? That somehow, by magic the problem would melt into the night? Who has not gone away on holiday hoping for utopia on their return? Who has not tried to go on pilgrimage to leave the problem at the holy shrine? Who has not discovered to their dismay, that if the problem resides within they carry it about – on the holiday, on the pilgrimage, and that it meets them fresh and alive on their return?

No, running away is no help. Problems do not melt into the night, yet for one in the depths of depression or insolvable pain and struggle both day and night can be intolerable. This was expressed well by Francis Thompson in his poem, The Hound of Heaven, when he said, "I said to dawn, be sudden, and to eve, be soon!" When suffering and sorrow visit us running away only lengthens the agony. Somehow, we must turn to the Lord for the wisdom and grace to receive these unwelcome visitors so that we may get to know them and prise their secret from them. If only we would turn to the Man of Sorrows, Jesus our Saviour, we would learn one of life's most enviable secrets, namely, that suffering and sorrow embraced with resignation to God's permissive will, and endured in cooperation with the redemptive work of Christ are merely joy and peace in disguise!

Everyone cries out for joy and peace, and so many cheap versions are on offer both in the spiritual supermarket, and indeed in secular society. There we are told that being insured up to one's eyeballs against everything that could possibly befall us will bring peace of mind. If so, why is our generation not a peaceful one? Why is there so much unhappiness? Why, when advertisements tell us that foreign holidays and new experiences will make us happy does joy seem to elude the majority?

We are told that the slim, healthy body, which is calmed by relaxation exercises, and exercised in sport, is happy. But where is the evidence for this? The slim, healthy calm exercised body asks what it is all *for* when the mind is agitated, and the meaning of life is not found, or disaster has struck on the sportsfield, in the gym or in the home. Society says that joy and peace are found in sex, and that this is so important, and so normal that there should be no rules to tie it down. If this is true why is there so much marriage breakdown? So much sex crime, even involving children? Why are prostitutes so unhappy? Why has the permissive society not found this elusive joy and peace, even though it craves for it? Since we are such a scientific people let us look at the evidence and conclude that we have searched in vain because we have looked to the wrong things, and reaped the wrong fruit. We have sowed the wind and reaped the whirlwind to our sorrow (Hos. 8.7).

The truth is that joy and peace are not for sale. They cannot be bought for money or arrived at through

physical exercises on mind or body. What is of the flesh is flesh. "It is the spirit that gives life, the flesh has nothing to offer" (John 6.63). Secular society cannot deliver on its promises, for joy and peace have nothing to do with materialism. They are two of the most precious gifts in the kingdom of God, and are given by the Lord to those who cooperate with Him in His plan to redeem them and the world.

There is a false peace and joy on offer through religion in general and spiritual movements also, where people think that without effort they should experience the peace that passes all understanding, and the joy that never fades (Phil. 4.7). Just because we carry out our religious duties does not mean that God owes us anything, for Jesus said: "When you have done all that you have been told to do, say, 'We are merely servants: we have done no more than our duty' " (Luke 16.10). There is a price to pay for joy and peace, which comes from embracing the cross, and allowing it to do its purifying work in our souls, cleansing us from the infection of sin and freeing us to walk as true daughters and sons of God.

It is not a passing euphoria that the Lord offers and there is no cheap grace. It is certainly not the "magic pill" on a spiritual level. The gifts of joy and peace are given at the price of the death of Jesus and His resurrection victory. They are not fizz that come and go. They are permanent gifts residing within one's innermost being. They are not given automatically, but have to be sought and found by those who are prepared to pay a price to achieve all that God offers, for "The Kingdom of God suffers violence, and the valiant take it by force" (Matt. 11.12).

The alternative is frightening. When we reject the

suffering that comes our way we expose ourselves to great trouble because it may break us and ruin our lives, leaving us locked permanently in bitterness, hatred, revenge, criminal behaviour or even madness. Some even lock themselves up in their homes or their rooms cut off from all life, not realizing that this self-inflicted punishment is worse than the original pain which could have been released. This is the breakdown side of the mystery where joy and peace are the breakthrough.

If we understand that joy and peace, coupled with agape-love are the most heavenly graces that we can experience: (in fact they are a foretaste of heaven): if we know this, then surely we would be wise enough to reach out for them? Just as the wealthy are prepared to pay enormous sums to buy a work of art that has only temporal value, would we not be prepared to "pay" a little in terms of embracing suffering in order to experience the kingdom of God on earth? Or have we fallen victims to materialism to the point of becoming atheistic too? Are we victims to the passing pleasures of the earth to the point that we do not see that all humanity cries out for the secret of joy and peace coupled with love? St Paul says that the Kingdom of God IS righteousness, joy and peace in the Holy Spirit (Rom. 14.17).

Joy and peace are so heavenly that they cure the restlessness of the human heart, and we know that we have reached one of life's greatest goals. We have come to the place of rest, which is a symbol of the Promised Land (Heb. 3.7–4.11). When the heart comes to rest it brings great calm to both mind and body, which restores health, vigour and youthfulness to the person. We are given back our zest for life while realizing that the possibility of real holiness is within our grasp. We now come to understand Hebrews 12.2 which says that we should not "lose sight of Jesus, who leads us in our faith and brings it to perfection: for the joy that was still in the future, he endured the cross, disregarding the shamefulness of it, and from now on he has taken his place at the right of God's throne".

SUFFERING BRINGS JOY

Since we cannot escape the experience of sorrow and suffering, it is wise to learn how to benefit from it and put it to good use. However, we must first get over our resistance to the knowledge that suffering can have a meaning, and that it can be a valuable tool in our hands, and in the Lord's hands if taken seriously and used properly. The joy that Jesus saw ahead for Himself and all humanity is something that we find difficult to grasp.

Jesus knew that suffering was the lot of human beings, and he was not spared, for it came to him in many forms. He knew poverty from birth and all the disadvantages that poverty brings. He was a labourer who worked for a living with his hands, so he knew all about calloused hands, worn out bodies and the dishonesty of those who deal with labourers. He lacked the education and opportunities of the upper classes, and suffered the consequences all his life. This came against him when, as a travelling teacher he was despised and rejected by those who had passed through "the system", and who were, therefore, "official", teachers and preachers. He never gained acceptance from the "powers that be" who left him on the fringes of all "church" matters, but they envied his giftedness, and he suffered from their jealousy. Because they envied his popularity they tried to malign him with false accusations, accusing him of being a glutton and a drunkard while he lived on the roads as a permanent pilgrim with no money or anywhere to lay his head. They accused him of being possessed by the devil because they knew that this would damage his ministry and turn the people against him. As we read in Psalm 55 he suffered from their malicious tongues, and he too, was betrayed by one of his closest friends.

He was persecuted constantly by the Scribes and Pharisees who followed him everywhere picking holes in his teaching, and challenging his every word. They watched not only his personal conduct but that of his disciples, and since they envied their freedom with regard to the Law they attacked them at every turn. For Jesus it was like living under a microscope, and this must have created great pressure and stress. On top of all this Jesus suffered from "people pressure", as crowds came daily at all hours of the day and night to have their needs met with no thought for the Healer, and most of them had no concern for a return of gratitude or love. Most gave nothing in return for what they received. Only once Jesus complained of this gross selfishness which must have hurt him grievously, not so much for what it did to him, but for the damage that selfishness does to the selfish one. That occasion was when he healed ten lepers, but only one returned to give thanks. The others went about their business, and got on with life. It is very difficult to be constantly faced with the gross selfishness and demands of people who only want to be on the receiving end of life, and do not want to be transformed into life-givers themselves. They are still at the "give me" stage of drawing life from others. They are consumers who refuse to become producers. They remain part of the problem, and refuse to become part of the solution to life. As Jesus demanded a life-change in them they went away, some even turned against him. He was no longer Santa Claus handing out gifts for nothing, but a Redeemer interested in passing on life to the teeming masses of humanity.

As he illustrated in the healing of the Paralytic (Mark 2.1–12), taking away the body's problem is not the real issue. One can be paralysed and go to heaven: one can be healthy and go to hell. One can be paralysed and experience all the gifts and graces of the kingdom of God; one can achieve the fullness of holiness, so receiving back the use of the legs cannot be the REAL healing. We know that one can receive the healing of the body and refuse the grace of redemption at the same time. What use is it to gain the whole world and lose one's soul? It is very nice to be healed of paralysis, especially if you are the sick person, but we do them an extra injury if we insist that healing is the sign of God's working in them. For some, it is the patient bearing of the cross out of obedience to the permissive will of God, and in union with the sufferings of Jesus offered for the redemption of others that is the real grace and enlightenment. But many have lost sight of this wisdom today, and add great misery to the already heavy burden of the sick person, by giving them the impression that they are lacking in faith when they are not healed.

Or worse still, that their illness is due to sin, which may be the case as in the misuse of drink, drugs, sex, food or anything else we refuse to use with wisdom, understanding and knowledge. We all know that we can either eat or starve our way into illness, and the

same applies to drink or drugs, or the misuse of the body. But not all illness comes from misuse or sinfulness. Stress is the most conducive environment to illness, and that is a major problem today in society. Yet illness, in the end, is a mystery to be handled as best we can, rather than use it to judge others. Many a person has found grace and salvation through the experience of illness. The conversion of Saint Ignatius of Loyola is one public example.

THE CROSS OF JESUS

As the tide of public opinion turned against him Jesus faced the loneliness of one who has the solution to life that no one wants. It is like as if humans love their problems, they hold on to them so much. We fear to risk the new life that comes from embracing pain and suffering. There was nothing for it except to take up his own cross, make up of all the rejection, misunderstanding, spiritual blindness and refusal to live on the part of those he came to save. He had to shoulder the refusal of all of humanity to repent and live fully, and he did penance for the rest of us. He offered his suffering to his Father for the express purpose of opening the way for us to seek the wisdom and grace to do what we refused to do willingly.

"Father, forgive them; they do not know what they are doing" (Luke 23.34). This plea of the loving victim who gave his life for us reveals the true state of affairs, for when we hold on to our problems and refuse to face into them to solve them or learn from them; when we run away from sorrow and suffering, we don't realize that we are punishing ourselves by refusing the new life that comes through carrying one's cross bravely. In our refusal of grace we are being our own worst enemy, choosing death rather than life, for it is not possible to take a neutral position of non-choice. We either go forward or backward in life: we cannot sit on the fence, for non-life is death.

What Jesus proved is that resurrection can only come AFTER death. It cannot come before it. The price of resurrection is death, just as the price of the peace that passes all understanding that gives us permanent joy in the Lord can only come after sorrow and suffering have done their redemptive work in our lives. Joy and peace are the resurrection side of sorrow and suffering, and make one invincible in the area that has been conquered. Whatever it is that we have finally put at the foot of the cross and allowed to be fully redeemed, is then beyond the power of the enemy. It has passed over from death to life.

For example, if our pride has been permanently shattered through suffering, and we have with the help of divine grace brought it to the foot of the cross and let it die there, then the humility that is born is heaven-born and beyond the enemy's reach. It is resurrection, joy and peace. That person is gloriously free, and no insults will ever harm them again, for they are in the Lord's hands, and under the power of redemptive grace. We say this in that lovely prayer which is used as an acclamation after the consecration at Mass: "Lord, by your cross and resurrection you have set us free, you are the Saviour of the world." What Jesus wants is for this to become a lived reality in our lives, for then we become witnesses to the resurrection.

SUFFERING THAT GIVES LIFE

Jesus proved by his passion and resurrection that

suffering could be used in a redemptive way for others, for he offered his suffering to the Father, out of love for us, in order to free sinners from the slavery to sin and any bondage that prevented us from seeking and finding the Lord. When we suffer we have the option to do the same. We can use it fruitfully for our own redemption or that of others, or both.

Let me illustrate with a story from Saint Maximilian Kolbe's life: during his stay in Auschwitz concentration camp he was kicked almost to death by one of the guards just because he was a priest. He was left for dead, but the other prisoners took him back to the barracks. As soon as he recovered consciousness he said: "I offer this suffering for the salvation of that man, Lord". It was needless violence, but if he had to undergo it, he was wise enough not to let it be for no reason. He deliberately gave it value, and took his place at the Saviour's side as a co-redeemer, something we all have many opportunities to do, if only we would collect the sorrows and sufferings of life and use them. Maximilian, as we know, ended his glorious ministry by laying down his life to save a man he hardly knew.

LIGHT AT THE END OF THE TUNNEL

Before we take up the question of suffering for others, let us see what it will do for ourselves when we let it work for us. Sorrow and suffering, no matter what their source, whether they come from personal problems, family heartbreak, tragedy or any other source, have the same effect if we let it work. First of all it forces us to think deeply about life. It kills superficiality dead, along with those easily picked up notions about life that do not stand up to the test. Strongly held opinions, which were really only mental structures to give a semblance of security and peace of mind, topple with the rest leaving us feeling very vulnerable and realizing, maybe for the first time, that our "Christianity" is rather skin deep. Was there any reality beyond the religious cliches we used so easily? Our prayer sounds hollow now even to ourselves, and the "Good God" we knew may have disappeared completely into the darkness, leaving us alone, frightened, feeling very exposed spiritually and emotionally.

For the first time we may be ready to glimpse a little of that darkness that made Jesus cry out from the cross: "My God, my God, why have you forsaken me? (Matt. 27.46). The first cry of the one plunged into suffering is "WHY? why! why should it happen to me? What have I done to deserve this? Is God punishing me?" We must not intervene to answer the question, which would be useless anyway, as they would not hear when the wound is fresh. This is the beginning of the journey, so just help them to take their place at the foot of the cross, where they have been invited to enter into the mystery of suffering and death, which can be transformed into joy and peace in the new life of the resurrection, if they persevere. They have been called to participate in the Paschal Mystery, not as spectators, but as participators, which is a great privilege, although the beginner can be forgiven for not believing us! After all, we are looking back from the vantage point of experience and they have just entered the darkness. It is the same with one who is about to undergo a serious operation: the fact that you may have survivednsuch an operation does not take away one iota of the fear or danger that the present patient experiences. Your reassurance does not take the pain away, and they must go on alone into the night of suffering. It is a known

fact that a "minor operation" always happens to someone else: the major operation is what happens to us! Let us take them by the hand, gently, therefore, until they see for themselves that there is light at the end of the tunnel.

THE FOOT OF THE CROSS

It would be a great help, of course, if we could make friends with those other participators at the foot of the cross, who can teach us and strengthen us for the journey ahead. John's gospel tells us that Jesus' mother was there as the queen of martyrs. All mothers and martyrs, whether called to shed their blood in red martyrdom or the white martyrdom of mental and emotional crucifixion, can find solace in her suffering. Mary of Magdala was there too, and all sinners can find solace in her, while all innocent victims can go to the Beloved Disciple standing faithfully beside his Master through terrible circumstances. There were other women there to give their compassion and motherly care to all those forgotten souls whose suffering goes unnoticed by everybody. No matter who we are there is a place for us at the foot of the cross. There is comfort too, strength, help and above all divine grace. It is foolish to think that we can handle the journey from any other starting point. The friends of Jesus were there too, a little further back from the cross. They will be there for the sufferer too, both for ministry and for intercessory prayer.

Let us not be afraid of the darkness, but go into it bravely with our hands in those of Jesus and His friends. One of the first lessons in this school of suffering – for that is what we have entered unknown to ourselves – is that of our own sinfulness. We listen to ourselves react to these circumstances with anger, despair, bitterness, unforgiveness, maybe even a desire for revenge, and we want to hit out at God for allowing it to happen. Human nature feels it has the right to a trouble-free existence, yet experience teaches that only in the school of suffering do we grow to maturity spiritually and emotionally. How unwilling we are to grow! How few of us are prepared to give Job's response to unmerited suffering: "If we take happiness from God's hand, must we not take sorrow too?" (Job 2.10).

It was Job's response that showed that he was a just man. It is our response to sorrow and suffering that reveals our innermost thoughts, and shows us and others the spiritual condition of our souls. When suffering refuses to go away quickly, then a deeper furrow is made in us, revealing the innate sinfulness of human nature more deeply. We may have been prepared to rise to the occasion once to forgive heroically, but constant forgiveness is another matter. Very few people consider Jesus' injuction to forgive seventy times seven as more than a theoretical illustration. Yet life demands constant forgiveness from many people where, for example, a spouse refuses to change a pattern of behaviour that is destroying a family. Since one cannot force that change on the other forgiveness is the way to peace in the midst of the storm.

THE WAY OUT

Sorrow and suffering show up our deep-seated selfishness, our pride and our stubborness. We have to face our own touchiness, and quick anger in words and deeds to others. Many people who suffer *want* someone else to feel their pain and they inflict pain on those nearest to them, or they become sullen, negative and uncooperative. What are we to do? The choice now is depression, despondency and despair, or turn to the Lord for redemption and healing. Our sense of sinfulness on top of everything else can be just too much to bear, but the Lord has provided the way out. It is in Psalm 130.

> Out of the depths I cry to you, O Lord,
>> Lord, hear my voice!
> O let your ears be attentive
>> to the voice of my pleading.

> If you, O Lord, should mark our guilt,
>> Lord, who would survive?
> But with you is found forgiveness:
>> for this we revere you.

Here the psalmist tells us to cry out to God from the depths of our despair, hopelessness, need, pain, etc. Name whatever it is that is causing the deepest grief . . . "from the depths of my sinfulness, I cry to you, O Lord!" So we have come to the foot of the cross and named the problem to the only one who can save us. Then we beg Him to listen, as we beg doctors, family or friends to LISTEN, to HEAR us. We let the Lord know that our sins block the way to Him and he alone can unblock our passage by His heroic and all-embracing forgiveness, which makes us reverence and adore Him for His unmerited love. He alone can give us peace, and the first peace is His forgiveness, for he knows that the spirit is willing but the flesh is weak.

My soul is waiting for the Lord,
   I count on his word.
My soul is longing for the Lord
   more than watchman for daybreak . . .

Because with the Lord there is mercy
   and fullness of redemption,
Israel indeed he will redeem
   from all its iniquity.

Having named our problem we then take our place at the foot of the cross and await the transformation that redemption brings. Since it is not an instant transformation which we ourselves nor those we live with could cope with, we need to be patient with the slow work of God that will, in the end, change us out of recognition, because it will transform us into the mind and heart of Christ. But don't worry about being noticed! Human beings are so self-centred that you will be very far gone in sanctity before anyone notices, even those who live with you. So cheer up!

Amazing as it may seem but all this self-knowledge leads to a long period of repentance and inner cleansing that prepares the soul for a deeper union with the Lord. There is no greater instrument than suffering to reveal to us our urgent need of inner cleansing so that it becomes possible for us to really do God's will in our lives. In other words a time of suffering and sorrow is a mine of self-knowledge if only we were teachable and let God work with us. If we face the self-knowledge and get spiritual help, I guarantee you that an exciting new life will open up that will change everything for the good, as St Paul tells us in Romans 8.28, where he says that God cooperates with all those that love Him by turning everything to their good. That "everything" includes all the suffering and sorrow that threatens to destroy us. It is important to emphasize that it is only when handed over to God that it will turn out to the good.

This is so even when we are not healed, or the problem remains unchanged, as in the case of marriage breakdown where the other partner has re-married. No matter how you react you are still cast aside by your partner. As also in the case of the death of a beloved one, for they remain dead no matter how you deal with your bereavement. The case is the same for a family member who seems to be impervious to grace, and so the agony goes on for you. We don't offer you magic, but the good news that there is a way out. You don't have to be imprisoned in your problem.

SUFFERING AS TEACHER AND ENLIGHTENER

Once we allow suffering to teach us, the burden is already lighter, and the tunnel is no longer completely dark. There is both life and light at the end of the tunnel, and suffering is the great teacher who makes us experts in the art of living. If suffering did nothing else but become our teacher and enlightener, is it not useful, although painful? Would it not be more tragic to go further into life with the spiritual blindness you had up to the moment when sorrow struck? How often have we heard sick people in hospital say: "I wasn't a good person, but since I got sick I have been thinking about my life, and now I want to do something about it" . . . or words to that effect. That sickness is not evil when it is a gilt-edged invitation to find life and find the Lord at a deeper level before it is too late. Once we begin to look at things from the Lord's perspective sorrow and suffering are not what people say they are. They are good, wholesome, albeit unwelcome friends.

As we proceed through the school of suffering learning the many lessons taught by those teachers of life, sorrow and suffering, we are not only enlightened about life issues and truth but we are cleansed of the effects of sin that cling so easily to us, especially the clinging self. Psalm 51 expresses this very well:

> Have mercy on me, God, in your kindness.
> In your compassion blot out my offence.
> O wash me more and more from my guilt
> and cleanse me from my sin.

The only way to become permanently free of the destructive effects of sorrow and suffering is to let the searing fire of God touch our innermost being. The burning coal that touched Isaiah's lips purified him (Isa. 6.7), but the fire of the Holy Spirit must burn our innermost being to make it a fit dwelling place for the Lord. John the Baptist warned us of this when he said that Jesus would baptize us in the Holy Spirit AND FIRE (Matt. 3.11). And that fire is first of all suffering, the ordinary things of everyday life that cause us pain, but also the great problems and tragedies that threaten us deeply, the fiery trials of life.

LET GO AND LET GOD

Sorrow and suffering not only cleanse us but also detach us from material things and our clinging to what is temporal and ephemeral. As such they are the perfect teachers to prepare us for death, which is the final letting go of the temporal for the eternal, the final

death that leads to freedom and life that lasts forever. The first death is letting the mountains of pride, arrogance, selfishness, lust, be toppled and the valleys of our fears, hopelessness, depressions, and despair be filled with healing, hope, faith and love, and thus that great prophecy of Isaiah 40.1–5 is fulfilled personally in us.

"Console my people, console them says your God. Speak to the heart of Jerusalem and call to her that her time of service is ended, that her sin is atoned for, that she has received from the hands of the Lord double punishment for all her crimes. A voice cries, 'prepare in the wilderness a way for the Lord. Make a straight highway for our God across the desert. Let every valley be filled in, and every mountain and hill laid low, let every cliff become a plain, and the ridges a valley; then the glory of the Lord will be revealed and all mankind will see it; for the mouth of the Lord has spoken'".

INNER STRENGTH

Thus we are cleansed and strengthened from within. Suffering borne in union with Christ brings enormous inner strength and fortitude, which I call "steel for your soul". When these great steel girders are made within, then a great spiritual edifice can be built for God and it will withstand the storms of life (see Matt. 7.24–27). Believe it or not, but the day will come when you will thank God for the privilege of entering the mysterious School of Suffering – which is also the School of the Holy Spirit. Let us turn again to St Paul in Romans 8.17 where he says that if we ARE children of God, then we are "heirs as well: heirs of God and coheirs with Christ, sharing His suffering so as to share His glory".

As we allow the Lord to work with us and within us he reveals Himself very personally and calls us to the full union of mind and heart with Him that is the resurrection joy and peace, which can only be experienced by one doing the whole will of God. This purifying, cleansing stage of suffering is very private, and very much an inner experience that calls for silence and solitude in one's day. Sometimes we call this silence "space" or "mind-time", the space to be and become, and the time to think in peace and make life-decisions. This is essential for the healing to take place under the very noses of those we live with, yet unobserved by all. At this stage many fear they will become overly religious and stand out like a sore thumb. The contrary is true, because this purification heals us of all piousity, and religious cliches, and we learn the true meaning of words and deeds. We become quiet and tranquil and *this* others will notice, without knowing why. If you are wise you will keep a closed mouth on the King's secret for fear of giving an opening to the enemy of our souls who would delight in increasing our pain from the misunderstanding of well-meaning good people. Let us obey Psalm 141.3: "Lord, set a guard over my mouth, a watcher at the gate of my lips".

INNER PEACE AT LAST

This first real taste of inner peace is so precious a grace that now you become a special soul. Others would like the gift but without paying the price. Gratitude, one of the purest sentiments of the human heart, is born. It now wells up from our innermost being to give praise to God for no other reason than that He IS God. This is REAL religion. It is now that you begin to appreciate

42

that the dark tunnel of suffering that you thought was the *tomb* of your life was, in fact, the *womb* from which emerged a precious new life, full of resurrection grace and glory and it is all the Lord's work. The fruits of this life will be all of grace, literally heaven-born, emitting the odour of The Beloved to you and to all those you live with (see Gal. 5.16–24 esp. v. 22).

From this point suffering and sorrow can no longer be seen as an evil, or destructive, since they are so life-giving. They have taken us by the hand and brought us into the very heart of the paschal mystery, where death emerges into life; failure gives way to victory, and darkness to light. When we emerge we bless God for the wounds that now glitter in the light of Heaven for we have been transformed into another Christ. "Death where is your victory? Death, where is your sting? Now the sting of death is sin . . . Let us thank God for giving us the victory through our Lord Jesus Christ" (I Cor. 15.55–57).

My friend, do not be afraid to go into the tomb with Jesus, for Paul says again in Romans 6.5–11 that if, "in union with Christ we have imitated his death, we shall also imitate him in his resurrection. We must realize that our former selves have been crucified with him to destroy this sinful body and to free us from the slavery of sin . . . we believe that having died with Christ we shall return to life with him . . . " so that the life we live is literally *in* Christ (see Col. 3.1–3).

Thus we see that sorrow and suffering are a major factor in our own redemption. Since this is so we cannot look at them as evil but as the messengers of joy and peace and a radiance that is heaven-born. In this regard we can look at the word that Jesus spoke to Martha in John 11.40: "Have I not told you that *if* you believe you *will* see the glory of God?". The opposite of this is to refuse to accept that suffering and sorrow come to bring us to the Promised Land. Because we refuse to believe neither do we see the glory of God work out in our lives. How sad! For you have to bear the suffering anyway, but now it is useless to you or anyone else. As such it *can* be a destructive force in your life to bring you down. Beware!

REDEMPTIVE SUFFERING

At the Last Supper, when Jesus instituted the Eucharist "he took some bread, and when he had said the blessing he broke it and gave it to them 'Take It', he said, 'this is my body'. Then he took the cup, and when he had returned thanks he gave it to them, and all drank from it, and he said to them, 'This Is My Blood, the blood of the covenant which is to be poured out for many. I tell you solemnly, I shall not drink any more wine until the day I drink the new wine in the Kingdom of God' " (Mark 14:22–25).

When Jesus consecrated the bread and changed it into his body, he challenged his disciples to *take it*, and all that it represented in terms of the broken, but afterwards resurrected body of the Lord. To participate in the Eucharist is to participate in the entire mystery of the death and resurrection of the Lord (see 1 Cor. 11.27). It means to align oneself completely with Jesus, the Saviour of all humankind. While we receive the fruits of his death and resurrection we are challenged to become participators also. It is not enough to *celebrate* Eucharist, we must *become* Eucharists, other Christs whose lives are given for others in service, even to the

laying down of the life (John 15.13). Our lives should be a source of life for others.

Jesus took the cup – which normally signifies a cup of suffering in the Bible – and St Mark says that they *all* drank from it. To become participators in the Paschal Mystery is to drink the cup of suffering. Jesus went straight from the supper to his passion and death. The Apostles, disciples and friends of Jesus all participated in it with varying levels of response, from betrayal in Judas, to denial in Peter, to desertion in the other male disciples: from utter faithfulness from Jesus' mother and the women disciples to that of John the Beloved male disciple, the faithful one.

When the Apostles moved out into public ministry after Pentecost they soon found that they had to drink the cup of suffering daily, as persecution was to be their lot as representatives of Jesus (see Acts 4, 5, 6, 7, 8.1–8, 9.1 – 2, 16 – 17, etc.). By then they had learned some of the lessons of the passion of Jesus, so they endured suffering joyfully, considering it an honour to suffer for the Lord (Acts 5.40–41). During the passion they had observed how Jesus responded. They saw him behave lovingly to his betrayer in Gethsemane, and with great concern and love towards Peter in his fall, apparently unconcerned about his own fate. They saw his patience and silence with his torturers; his loving concern for his mother, and his incredible response to the Good Thief. These unforgettable scenes burned their way into their souls and inspired their own future behaviour.

When Jesus was tried unjustly on false charges, accused by false witnesses and condemned by the High Priest and those representing all religious matters: when all the rules for a just court-case were put aside, and against the Law he was condemned by something he was forced to say: when he was maltreated by the guards, mocked and jeered . . . they saw no negativity! He did not REACT to that dreadful situation, but RESPONDED with respect for those in authority and with forgiveness to all. There was no anger, resentment or bitterness to be found in him for his dreadful fate, as we are tempted to express. There was only loving acceptance of this injustice which he freely offered to the Father for the redemption of us all.

He knew that he could transform the base metal of suffering into the gold of redemption, and we, too, can do it in him and through him. Therefore, he accepted the robe of mockery so that, one day, we would wear the robe of righteousness on earth, and the robe of glory in Heaven. He accepted the crown of thorns so that we would wear a crown of glory in Paradise. He accepted captivity and death so that he could set free the *real* captives, those who are enslaved to sin and death and are therefore in danger of seeing *real* death, which is absence from God, or Hell (see Luke 4.18). He accepted torture to free us from the final torture in Hell. *Therefore, He loves us!*

Like ourselves, the Apostles needed to see this glorious testimony to heroic love so that they could make spiritual treasure out of the suffering they had to endure anyway! Afterwards when they were flogged by the Sanhedrin they knew that it was a privilege to offer this pain, in union with Jesus for the salvation of souls. The offering made in this way carries the infinite merits of Jesus, the Redeemer, and becomes our drop of water put into the wine of His saving love for others. Suffering is no longer an empty endurance, but a triumphant endurance.

THE CHRISTIAN AND THE CROSS

Once Jesus transformed suffering and gave it redemptive value, it became an altogether new experience. He made it perfectly clear that His disciples and followers would suffer persecution for His sake, and that in every age. Not only were we not to fall or fail under the lash, but He told us to use this experience as an opportunity to witness to our faith. "Be on your guard: they will hand you over to sanhedrins (religious bodies); you will be beaten in synagogues (where you would expect acceptance and love for God); and you will stand before governors and kings (civil bodies) for my sake, *to bear witness before them* since the Good News must . . . be proclaimed to all the nations" (Mark 13.9–10). In fact things would get so bad that the pressure of persecution would make family members betray one another even to death (Mark 13.12–13). He said that we would "be hated by all men on account of my name . . . " (Mark 13.13).

Truly it is imperative for Christians to delve deeply into the mystery of redemptive suffering since the cross has been laid on the back of the Church as it was laid on Jesus' back. Besides, the Church *is* the Mystical Body of Christ, and it continues the mission of Christ in the world today. Jesus passed on His mission to us, and that includes suffering. But we are never alone because He is the Head of the Body (Col. 1.18), and His merits give value to our suffering for Him beyond our ability to measure.

It is a well-known axiom that the blood of the martyrs is the seed of the Church, and Church history bears abundant witness to the fact that persecution does not diminish her in any way but instead occasions fresh growth in the Spirit. We are therefore challenged to look on suffering for Christ in a way that the unbelieving world would not comprehend. When we suffer persecution for Jesus we are experiencing the Paschal Mystery in our own lives, and that is the mystery of redemption which saves souls. It is utter privilege, even if a painful one. Through it we are privileged to participate by God's grace in souls being reborn to the kingdom of God, and we become co-redeemers, although little ones. We stand *by* Jesus, *with* Jesus, *in* Jesus at the foot of the cross, and it is *through* Jesus that everything is accomplished. It is just our tremendous privilege to participate in the redemption of the world.

Our participation is done through prayer for the salvation of souls; through fasting freely undertaken for the same purpose, and by offering our sorrows and sufferings in union with our crucified and risen Lord, so that they are drenched with His merits, and thus become a power for salvation for others. Since we have to suffer let us not waste it since it can produce such divine fruit. There are people today unjustly imprisoned and tortured for their faith in different parts of the world. Instead of just languishing there in bitterness at their fate, so many of them are offering their sufferings in union with the merits of Jesus for the redemption of the country where they reside, as one of them said: "for the resurrection of our nation", and they are doing so with joy and peace even though their bodies are greatly troubled.

These are the great disciples of Jesus, who know how to walk in the Spirit and live a heavenly life on earth. They know experientially these words of Paul: "Let your thoughts be on heavenly things, not on the things that are on the earth, because you have died, and now the life you have is hidden with Christ in God. But when Christ is revealed – and he is your life – you too will be revealed in all your glory with him" (Col. 3.2–4).

DISCIPLES LIKE THE MASTER

The Acts of the Apostles and the New Testament letters make it clear that the early Christians were prepared to suffer for Christ, and that with joy "And so they left the presence of the Sanhedrin glad to have had the honour of suffering humiliation for the sake of the name" (Acts 5.41). Paul and Silas did not waste their night in prison in Acts 16.16–40: having been tortured unjustly and imprisoned they spent the night in the stocks, but also in prayer and praise, and occasioned a great miracle that converted even the jailer and his household. They did not waste their energy saying: "how can God be a good God and do that to me?" as so many do today, who seem to have lost the reality of the things of the Spirit and of walking in union with Jesus. It is such a great pity, for suffering must be an unbearable burden, and each sorrow visited upon them must be a crisis.

Even when St Paul was in his final imprisonment, chained to Roman soldiers night and day, facing execution for being a disciple of Christ, he still did not stop witnessing for the gospel: "My chains, in Christ, have become famous not only all over the Praetorium but everywhere, and most of the brothers have taken courage in the Lord from these chains of mine and are getting more and more daring in announcing the Message without any fear" (Phil. 1.13–14). Here he saw that his faithfulness to Jesus meant that the Mission

went on even though he himself was confined to barracks. He also saw that his courage inspired other Christians to go out and witness. The fact that he was confined to a house or prison made no difference to the spread of the gospel if only he would do what he could. This is an important message for all those imprisoned today, and also those who are housebound through illness or age or any other reason. Our confinement or disability is part of our offering to the Lord to be used for the salvation of the world, and our prayers must always be missionary.

Paul understood more than most the value of suffering for the spread of the gospel, and he had more than most to suffer too! If anyone ever understood "Take up your cross" it was he, and his letters bear testimony to this. Witness 2 Corinthians 4.7–11 and 16–18 where he lists some of the sufferings that he endured for the sake of Christ and the gospel: ". . . in difficulties on all sides, *but never cornered*; we see no answer to our problems, *but we never despair*; have been persecuted, *but never deserted*; knocked down, *but never killed* . . . consigned to death every day . . .". Notice the presence of the Lord invisibly through it all. The pain is great, but the power of the cross is great too, so great indeed, that Paul goes on to say that ". . . . though this outer man of ours may be falling into decay, the inner man is renewed day by day".

Like Jesus, Paul looked through the cross to the glory beyond and that enabled him to endure more, longer, joyfully (2 Cor. 11.21–29). In fact he weighs suffering in the balance with the glory beyond and finds it light, since the grace of Jesus' resurrection was there for him, as it is for us: "Yes, the troubles which are soon over, though they weigh little, train us for the carrying of a weight of eternal glory which is out of all proportion to them." It is a great liberation to come to this moment when suffering can be seen in the light of its divine fruit. It could be compared to the joy of a mother at the birth of her child when she instantly forgets the pain of labour. The new life obliterates the memory of the pain even when it was great.

PROOF OF CHRISTIANITY

Paul goes even further in 2 Corinthians 6.3–10 where he says that though we all claim to be Christians that few of us could *prove* it, because the proof lies in our willingness to endure suffering and sorrow for the Lord, and for the spread of His Kingdom: "Instead, we prove that we are servants of God by great fortitude in times of suffering: in times of hardship and distress; when we are flogged, or sent to prison, or mobbed; labouring, sleepless, starving . . . prepared for honour or disgrace, for blame or praise; taken for imposters while we are genuine; obscure yet famous; said to be dying and here we are alive; rumoured to be executed before we are sentenced; thought most miserable and yet we are always rejoicing; taken for paupers though we make others rich, for people having nothing though we have everything."

If the proof of discipleship lies here then we all have a lot to learn and to do for the Lord, and the material for serving God is all around us. It is there already in the circumstances of our lives, with its joys and sorrows, and with the great challenge to DO something for God and country with what we have. Let us take another look at our sufferings and decide never again to complain about our privileges! Perhaps God is taking

us more seriously than we realize? Perhaps he has been nudging us in the direction of making our lives fruitful for others instead of always taking care of number one? Wouldn't it be wonderful if you tested this out for yourself only to find yourself surprised by joy and a peace you did not think possible?

Look at the "junk" of your life and realize what a treasure it could be in the hands of the Lord . . . all those disappointments, heartbreaks, disillusionments, failures, illnesses, difficulties of all kinds, also those petty irritations that cause us to be impatient and bad-tempered . . . let us collect them all and begin to use them for the Kingdom and the salvation of souls. When we realize just how much we have to offer the Lord we will get busy in using our treasure. Just to begin with: are you praying for someone in need? How about salting your prayer with some little suffering which you will offer to the Lord *without complaint*, willingly and lovingly. Then see for yourself if the prayer is more powerful. Offer your great sufferings for the salvation of souls for that is the great request of the Our Father: Thy Kingdom come . . . to Mary or John or to our country.